ACKNOWLEDGEMENTS

I would like to extend my heartfelt gratitude to my husband, Antonio Bushell, whose unwavering support and encouragement were the pillars of strength throughout the creation of this book. Your patience, understanding, and belief in me sustained me through the long nights and endless revisions.

Thank you for being my rock, my sounding board, and my biggest cheerleader. Your love and encouragement fueled my creative spirit, and I couldn't have completed this journey without you by my side.

To my partner in life, who has shared in both the challenges and triumphs of this endeavor, thank you for always believing in me and for being the wind beneath my wings.

With all my love,

Nat Bushell

PROLOGUE

In the tranquil town of Hawthorne, nestled amid rolling hills and meandering streams, a tale of heartbreak and hope was about to unfold. It was a place where the sun painted golden hues upon the quaint houses, and the laughter of children echoed through the tree-lined streets. Hawthorne had always been more than just a town; it was a community of kindred spirits, a place where neighbors knew each other's names and shared life's joys and sorrows.

At the heart of this close-knit community was a spirited young girl named Emily. With her bright eyes and boundless enthusiasm, she embodied the innocence of childhood. Her days were often filled with laughter and adventure, exploring the world hand-in-paw with her loyal companion, Scooby. Together, they embarked on countless journeys, chasing butterflies, and discovering secret hideaways in the woods.

But life's serenity can be fleeting, and the bonds we hold dear can sometimes be tested in the harshest of ways. One fateful day, tragedy struck. The laughter that had once filled the air was silenced, and the warm embrace of Hawthorne's unity seemed to slip through the town's gentle fingers like grains of sand.

In the midst of a nation divided by the echoes of a recent election, the threads that had woven Hawthorne's fabric together began to unravel. Lines were drawn, friendships strained, and unity shattered. What had once been a town that worshipped together, supported one another, and celebrated life's triumphs, now found itself fractured and torn.

Yet, in the face of adversity, there lingered a glimmer of hope—a small but unwavering light that refused to be extinguished. It was Emily's resilience, her unwavering faith, and the memory of Scooby's unwavering love that would serve as the catalyst for change.

As Emily embarked on a journey to heal not only her own wounded heart but also the fractured soul of her community, she would discover the profound power of forgiveness, the unbreakable bonds of faith, and the ability of even the deepest of wounds to mend. Could a tragedy that had torn Hawthorne apart serve as a beacon of hope for the entire nation? Could this close-knit community find its way back to unity and rediscover the strength of their shared beliefs?

"Scooby's Gone" is a story of loss, redemption, and the resilience of the human spirit. It is a tale that reminds us that even in the darkest of times, the light of hope can guide us back to one another, helping us rediscover the power of love, faith, and forgiveness.

CHAPTER ONE

"Bonds of Love in Hawthorn"

In the quiet town of Hawthorn, nestled amidst rolling hills and lush greenery, lived the Henderson family. Emily, a bright-eyed and curious girl of twelve, was the heart of their home. Her parents, Matthew and Sarah, navigated the daily challenges of life with love and devotion.

One evening, as the sun dipped below the horizon, casting long shadows in their cozy bedroom, Emily's mother, Sarah, stood before the bathroom mirror, gently cleansing her face. On the other side of the room, Matthew sat hunched over the computer desk, engrossed in his work.

Sarah sighed, her reflection reflecting a sense of concern. "Honey, I just don't understand. Ever since this election, it feels like no one talks to each other anymore. It's so disturbing," she mused aloud. "Dan and Cindy haven't spoken to Paul or Vicky ever since they decided to vote for Truman. This election has caused so much division. Don't you think so?"

Matthew, absorbed in his task, continued typing, seemingly lost in thought.

"Honey, are you listening to me?" Sarah asked, her voice filled with worry.

Without looking up from the screen, Matthew replied, "Yes, honey, I'm just sending out this last email for tonight."

Sarah turned her attention back to her reflection, deep in thought. "Pastor Chad has been trying to think of ways to bring the Hawthorn Community back together again," she revealed, hoping to engage her husband in the conversation.

Finally hitting "send" on the email, Matthew walked over to Sarah in the bathroom. He playfully hugged her from behind, his lips brushing against her ear. "So, what plan did the Pastor come up with?" he teased.

Sarah chuckled, feeling her worries momentarily melt away. "I don't know," she admitted. "He talked about it, but I haven't heard anything else."

Matthew turned his wife to face him, their eyes locking. "It's going to take God and him alone to bring this community back together, let alone the nation after this last election," he said tenderly, leaning in to give her a gentle kiss.

Sarah pondered the situation. "So, what do you suppose should happen?" she asked, searching for answers.

Matthew sighed, his gaze locked onto his wife's eyes. "Your guess is as good as mine," he confessed. "But I do know that we can't go on like this as a community. We have to forgive one another because, at the end of the day, we all need each other, and something has to give."

As they shared this intimate moment in their dimly lit bedroom, the couple found solace in each other's presence, determined to contribute to their community's healing.

The night slowly faded away.

The following morning, as the sun gently caressed Hawthorn with its warm rays, Emily found herself in the midst of her morning routine in the bathroom. She brushed her teeth diligently, her ever-loyal companion, Scooby, playfully circling her.

"Scooby, I have to get ready for school. I'll play with you later," she said, smiling down at her furry friend.

Scooby sat down and whined, his big brown eyes pleading for attention. Emily finished brushing her teeth and left the bathroom, Scooby following closely behind. She knelt down beside him, her small hands folded in prayer.

"Dear God, please protect Scooby, my mother, father, and me today as I go off to school," Emily prayed earnestly. "Send forth your angels to protect us. Father, I pray Psalm 91 protection over my family and especially over Scooby."

She gently rubbed Scooby's head, his eyes reflecting gratitude for her love and care.

"I promise I'll play with you when I get home from school," she assured him.

Scooby barked happily, feeling reassured by her words.

From downstairs, Sarah called out, "Honey, you don't want to miss the bus! Hurry now!"

"I'm coming, Mom!" Emily responded with a grin. She turned to Scooby, her playfulness shining through. "See, Scooby, you're going to get me in trouble," she teased.

Scooby made a playful noise, his tail wagging in agreement. Emily grabbed her backpack and headed downstairs, Scooby tailing her like a faithful shadow.

As Emily's mother, Sarah, handed her daughter a packed lunch and homemade breakfast bars, their bond radiated warmth and love. Emily's heart swelled with gratitude.

"Thanks, Mom," Emily said, her smile lighting up the room.

"You're welcome, honey. Have a good day," Sarah replied, leaning in to kiss Emily on the cheek.

With her backpack slung over one shoulder, Emily walked to the door, waving goodbye to her mother. Sarah waved back, her heart full of love. Scooby sat beside Sarah, watching Emily as she boarded the school bus. Emily kept her gaze on her mother and Scooby until the bus disappeared down the street, leaving behind a sense of unity, love, and hope in their Hawthorn home.

CHAPTER TWO

"School Days and Friendship"

The school hallway buzzed with activity as students bustled to their respective classes. Emily, with her backpack slung over one shoulder, navigated through the sea of young minds and book-laden arms. She waved cheerfully at her teachers, Suzzette and Vicky, as they passed by.

"Hi Mrs. Weatherspoon," Emily greeted her teacher with a bright smile.

"Hi, Emily," Mrs. Weatherspoon replied warmly.

With a skip in her step, Emily entered her classroom and took her seat, ready to tackle another day of learning. As she settled in, her friend Cassey, a fellow student with a warm heart, approached her.

"Hey, Emily, how was church yesterday? I'm sorry I couldn't make it," Cassey inquired, concern lacing her words.

Emily, always eager to share her experiences, responded with enthusiasm. "No worries, Cassey. Church was great! My pastor taught forgiveness, from the book of Matthew, Chapter 6, verses 14-15."

She continued, her eyes bright with the lessons learned. "He said, 'For if you forgive other people when they sin against you, your heavenly Father will also forgive you. But if you do not forgive others their sins, your Father will not forgive your sins.'"

Cassey pondered Emily's words for a moment before breaking into a grin. "Is it okay if I don't forgive my brother for putting his stinky feet on my bed?" she quipped, a playful glint in her eye.

Emily laughed heartily at Cassey's remark, the two friends sharing a light-hearted moment.

Their jovial exchange was interrupted by their teacher, Mrs. Harrison, who called for attention. "Quiet up, class! Please turn in your homework assignments."

Students promptly made their way to the front of the classroom, depositing their completed assignments into the bin on Mrs.

Harrison's desk. She emphasized, "No horseplay, please."

As the clock on the wall signaled the end of the class, Emily found herself at her locker, packing up her belongings alongside Cassey. However, Cassey wore a troubled expression, and Emily couldn't help but notice.

"What's wrong?" Emily inquired, genuine concern in her voice.

Cassey sighed, her shoulders slumping as she spoke. "I bombed again in math. I got a D+. I don't think my mother is going to like this. She's always yelling at me, and I know this is going to make her dislike me even more."

Emily furrowed her brows, trying to understand. "What do you mean? Why do you think she's not going to like you?"

Tears welled up in Cassey's eyes as she admitted, "She repeatedly tells me it's my fault that my father left us."

Emily's heart ached for her friend. She reached out and gently placed a reassuring hand on Cassey's shoulder. "Cassey, you don't believe that, do you?"

Cassey hesitated for a moment, her voice quivering as she responded, "Sometimes I think it's true. She's never happy when I'm around, as if I'm this bad villain."

Emily shook her head vehemently. "That's not true, Cassey. You are an awesome person."

Cassey's eyes welled up with tears, and she managed a small, grateful smile. "Thank you, Emily."

Unable to contain her empathy, Emily pulled Cassey into a warm, comforting hug. "Aw, give me a hug," Emily said gently, offering her support.

As they embraced, Emily continued, "Do you think you'll be able to spend this weekend over at my house?"

Cassey, still teary-eyed but with a glimmer of hope, replied, "I don't know, Emily. Hopefully, but I'm not sure what my mom's going to say after she sees this D+."

CHAPTER THREE

Heartbreak on Hawthorn Street

As the school bus rumbled down Hawthorn Street, Emily stared out the window, lost in her thoughts. Her conversation with Cassey had left her pondering the complexities of family dynamics, and she couldn't help but worry about her friend.

Back at Emily's house, Scooby, their loyal and furry family member, eagerly awaited Emily's return. Unusually, her mother, Sarah, stood by the door without Scooby on his leash. It was as if he sensed her impending arrival and didn't want to miss a moment with Emily.

Inside the bus, Emily's mind was still occupied by her thoughts, causing her to be quieter than usual. She didn't notice the passing streets or the familiar landmarks on her route. Her focus remained on the weight of Cassey's struggles and the desire to be there for her friend.

Meanwhile, John, a troubled man battling his own demons, had been drowning his sorrows in alcohol. He was now behind the wheel, his tie loosened after a long, stressful day at work. Drunk and reckless, he sped down the road, heading in the direction of Emily's street.

Unaware of the impending danger, Emily's bus continued on its route. As she drew closer to home, her thoughts shifted back to her dear Scooby and the joy he brought to her life. She couldn't wait to see him again.

Back at the house, Sarah's anxiety grew as she anticipated Emily's arrival. Scooby, too, seemed to sense her approaching return and grew increasingly eager to greet her. However, today was different; Sarah didn't have him on his leash as she usually did.

As the bus approached Emily's street, John's erratic driving brought him dangerously close to disaster. He was inebriated and speeding, heading straight for Hawthorn Street. His blurred vision made it difficult to navigate, and he failed to notice the approaching school bus.

In the midst of this chaos, Scooby couldn't contain his excitement any longer. He darted toward the door, eager to welcome Emily back home.

Sarah, realizing that Scooby was about to run out, cried out in panic, "Scooby, get back here!"

Emily, still lost in her thoughts, was momentarily jolted from her reverie when she heard her mother's frantic voice. "Scooby!"

Scooby reached the curb just as the school bus pulled up. At that exact moment, John, the drunk driver, veered onto Hawthorn Street, crossing over the curb and onto the sidewalk.

A collective gasp filled the air as the unthinkable happened. John's vehicle struck Scooby with a sickening thud before continuing its reckless course, leaving behind a scene of chaos and heartbreak.

Emily, who had just disembarked from the bus, witnessed the horrifying incident unfold in slow motion. She saw Scooby being hit, and her world seemed to crumble around her.

Mourning screams filled the air as Sarah raced toward the street, her heart pounding with dread. Emily fell to the ground beside Scooby, her tears flowing freely as she cradled her beloved companion.

"No, Scooby, please don't die! Please, Scooby, don't die!" Emily cried out in anguish, her voice filled with pain and desperation.

Onlookers gathered around, their faces marked with disbelief and sorrow. The hit-and-run driver, John, continued on his reckless path, leaving behind a shattered family and a heartbroken girl in his wake.

Hawthorn Street was forever changed on that fateful day, as the community grappled with the tragic loss of one of its own.

CHAPTER FOUR

Broken Dreams

The dimly lit garage was shrouded in an eerie silence as John clumsily steered his dented car into its familiar spot. He cursed under his breath as he assessed the damage, blaming Scooby for the mishap.

"Stupid dog," John muttered, his voice dripping with frustration. He stumbled out of the car and made his way to the front right side, examining the dent with a scowl etched across his face.

Inside the house, Suzzette was busy in the kitchen when she heard the garage door. She wondered why John was home so early, and her concern grew when she heard him stumble into the house.

"Honey, is there a reason why you're home so early?" Suzzette inquired, worried evident in her voice.

John's reply was a slurred mumble. "I finished up early today. Can I do that?"

Suzzette's concern deepened. She had seen this pattern before, and it never led to anything good. "John, have you been drinking again?" she asked, her voice tinged with apprehension.

John's temper flared, and he snapped, "Susan, why all the questions? Geez!"

Suzzette took a step closer, her concern unwavering. "John, I thought we talked about this. How many drinks did you have?"

"I only had a couple of drinks, that's it!" John retorted, his voice growing louder and more agitated.

Suzzette wasn't convinced. "John, you can't keep going on like this. When are you going to get some help?"

"Susan, I told you I don't need any help," John snapped back. "I'll be just fine. I just need to sleep this off."

Suzzette sighed, tears welling up in her eyes. "I hope you know that your drinking pushed Johnnie away," she said softly.

This accusation struck a nerve in John, and he lashed out. "How dare you, excuse me for pushing that boy away. I didn't push anyone away; he pushed himself away. Maybe your nagging pushed him away. Did you ever think about that, Susan? I did everything for that boy, but yet that wasn't good enough."

Suzzette felt tears streaming down her face as John's anger flared. His temper intensified, and he grabbed her face forcefully, causing her to recoil in fear.

"I better not ever hear you say some nonsense out of your mouth like that ever again, you hear me!" John threatened, his eyes filled with rage.

Suzzette, shaken and startled, moved his hands off her face and fled the room.

"I'm nothing like my Father," John yelled after her. "Johnnie will come home to visit someday once he gets some sense in his head. I can't believe you said I act like my Father."

John's anger boiled over, and he struck the wall in frustration, the impact echoing through the empty room.

CHAPTER FIVE

Whispers in the Dark

Night had fallen over Hawthorn Street, casting a shadow of grief and despair. In Emily's bedroom, her mother lovingly tucked her into bed. Emily's tear-stained face revealed the pain of losing Scooby, her beloved friend.

"Mom," Emily whispered through her tears.

Her mother sat down beside her, a soothing presence in the dimly lit room. "Yes, honey?"

Sobbing softly, Emily poured out her heart. "Scooby's gone, and I'm going to miss him so much."

Her mother tenderly stroked Emily's hair and brushed away a stray tear. "I know, honey. I'm going to miss him too."

"Why didn't the person just stop?" Emily asked, her voice quivering with sadness and confusion.

Her mother sighed, struggling to find the right words to comfort her grieving daughter. "I don't know, honey."

Emily clung to her mother's presence, seeking solace in her love and warmth. "Mom?"

"Yes, sweetheart?" her mother replied, her own eyes filled with sorrow.

"Why did God let this happen to Scooby?" Emily's voice trembled as she questioned her faith. "I prayed for his protection this morning."

Her mother held Emily close, her heart aching for her daughter's pain. "Honey, God didn't let this happen to Scooby, you hear me. God had nothing to do with this. Honey, let's finish talking about this in the morning. I need you to get some rest. It's been a very long day."

With a gentle kiss on Emily's forehead, her mother hoped to offer some semblance of comfort in the midst of their heartbreak. Yet, both mother and daughter knew that the pain of Scooby's loss would linger far beyond this dark and tearful night.

As Mother left Emily's room, she gave her one last loving glance, cherishing the bond between them. Emily's tearful eyes spoke volumes about her heartache over losing Scooby, her cherished companion.

"Love you, honey," Mother whispered softly before heading toward the bedroom door.

"Love you too, Mom," Emily replied, her voice trembling with a mixture of sadness and gratitude for her mother's comforting presence.

Mother offered a reassuring smile before gently closing the bedroom door, leaving Emily in the quiet darkness of her room. As the door clicked shut, Emily couldn't help but feel the weight of her loss.

Downstairs, in the dimly lit living room, Mother found herself lost in thought. She knew that her daughter was grieving, but there was little she could do to ease Emily's pain. With a sigh, she whispered, "Goodnight," as she headed toward the living room.

"Goodnight, Mom," Emily replied, her voice barely audible from her bedroom.

As Mother descended the stairs, a sudden and unexpected ring of the doorbell shattered the silence of the house. Father Matthew, who had been sitting in the living room, watching the evening news, rose from his chair and walked to the front door. He greeted the two police officers who stood on the doorstep, their expressions somber.

"Hello, come in," Father Matthew offered, stepping aside to allow the officers entry.

"Thank you," Officer Kirk replied as they entered the house.

Once inside, the police officers took out a pencil and notepad, ready to address the matter at hand. Father Matthew could sense the seriousness of the situation as he welcomed them into their home.

"How are you all holding up?" Officer Peterson asked, offering his condolences.

Matthew replied, "We're all holding up, okay. It's a very unfortunate tragedy losing Scooby. Scooby was part of our family. We got him when Emily was just a little baby."

The officers expressed their sympathy, acknowledging the pain that came with such a loss. With empathy in their eyes, they inquired, "Can you tell us what happened?"

Sarah, who had joined Matthew by the door, exchanged a glance with him. She hesitated for a moment but then spoke up, "Well, I was at the door with Scooby, getting ready to go outside. Scooby and I usually wait until Emily's bus arrives, and we go out to meet her. This particular time, Scooby ran out ahead of me. He was at the curb, as I was running after him, yelling his name. The bus was coming, and this car was driving so fast it ran up on the curb and hit Scooby. It happened so fast."

Mother's voice quivered as she recounted the traumatic incident. Father Matthew, seeing the pain in her eyes, put a comforting arm around her.

"He just kept on driving," Mother continued, her voice breaking. "I thought he would at least stop, but he didn't."

The officers listened attentively, making notes as Mother spoke. It was evident that the hit-and-run incident had deeply affected her and the entire family.

"Were you able to get any information on the vehicle? Possibly the make, model, or color of the vehicle?" Officer Kirk inquired.

Sarah shook her head, her eyes filled with sorrow. "No, the vehicle was going so fast I wasn't able to make out anything on the vehicle."

Officer Peterson asked, "Have you seen that vehicle around here before?"

Sarah looked at her husband and replied, "No, not that I could recall."

Officer Kirk continued his questioning. "Were you able to see the driver?"

Again, Sarah's response was filled with sadness. "No, I wasn't able to see the driver. But I do know that whoever was driving that car was driving like a bat out of hell. I'm so glad there weren't any kids out there at the time."

The officers nodded, taking down all the information they could gather. As they continued their investigation, Sarah and Matthew exchanged concerned glances, knowing that their family had been forever changed by the tragic loss of Scooby. Unanswered questions lingered in the air, and they couldn't help but wonder if justice would ever be served for their beloved companion.

The officers concluded their conversation with Mr. and Mrs. Stephenson, thanking them for their cooperation.

"Well, thank you for your time, Mr. and Mrs. Stephenson. This is all the information we will need at this time," Police Officer 1 stated.

Matthew responded, "You're welcome. We hope we've been helpful."

Officer Peterson chimed in with gratitude, saying, "You have been more than helpful. Thank you."

Mrs. Stephenson's eyes were filled with determination as she voiced her concerns, "We need to hurry in finding this person and get this reckless person off of the streets as quickly as possible before they kill someone else."

Officer Kirk nodded in agreement. "And that's what we're going to get busy working on. Again, we're so sorry about what happened to your dog, Scooby. We will investigate this and try to find out who did this and help get some justice for Scooby."

"Thank you both so much," Mrs. Stephenson expressed her gratitude.

Officer Kirk added, "We have some K-9s at the station. If you would like to someday bring Emily down to the station to visit, we would be glad to have her."

Mrs. Stephenson smiled appreciatively. "Thanks for the offer. I'm sure she would love that."

Matthew extended his hand to the officers, saying, "Thanks for your help."

Officer Peterson shook his hand with a friendly nod. "You're welcome. It was a pleasure."

With their conversation concluded, the police officers made their way out, and Matthew closed the door behind them. However, their peaceful evening was soon disrupted as Emily began screaming from her bedroom. Both parents rushed to her side, concerned for their daughter.

"Honey, are you okay?" Matthew asked, his voice filled with worry.

They hurried to Emily's bed, where Mother sat down and wrapped her arms around their trembling daughter. Emily was in distress, caught in the throes of a nightmare.

"It's okay, honey," Mother reassured her, her soothing voice attempting to comfort Emily.

"Daddy and I are both here. Everything's going to be alright. You had a bad dream."

Emily moaned softly as she clung to her mother. "Scooby's gone, Mommy."

Mother exchanged a glance with Matthew before turning her attention back to their daughter. "Yes, Scooby's gone, but we'll get through this, I promise. We have everyone praying for us. Pastor Chad called to check on you, and he'll be by tomorrow. Cassey called and said she wanted to see how you were doing."

Mother leaned down and kissed Emily's forehead, hoping to bring some solace to their grieving daughter.

CHAPTER SIX

Community, Compassion, and Challenges

The next day at school, Suzzette and her best friend Vicky discussed the tragic incident that had befallen Emily's beloved dog, Scooby.

Suzzette sighed deeply, her sympathy evident in her voice. "I feel so sorry for what happened to Emily's dog, Scooby. That's so tragic."

Vicky nodded in agreement, her expression mirroring the sorrow in her friend's eyes. "I know. I feel so bad for her. I heard Scooby was running out to meet Emily at the bus stop like he normally does, and a car ran over the curb and hit the poor dog."

The two friends shared a moment of somber reflection, empathizing with the pain Emily must be going through during this difficult time.

Suzzette and Vicky continued their conversation about the tragic incident involving Emily's beloved dog, Scooby. The two friends shared a sense of disbelief and anger over the heartless act that had taken Scooby's life.

"Whoever did this was a monster," Suzzette remarked, her voice filled with indignation. "To hit Scooby and keep going as if nothing ever happened. That had to be a cold-blooded person with no heart."

Vicky nodded in agreement, her thoughts mirroring Suzzette's. "That's exactly what I was thinking. At least the person could have stopped. They should have heard some kind of thump. I remember the day Emily brought Scooby to school. He was so fun to be around.

All the kids loved him; they couldn't stop petting him."

Suzzette and Vicky shared a fond memory of Scooby's visit to school, both of them smiling at the recollection. "Yeah, I remember that day," Suzzette sighed. "Scooby was so friendly to everyone."

Vicky brought up the recent community response to Scooby's tragic passing. "Did you see all the flyers posted all around town?"

Suzzette admitted that she hadn't noticed any flyers earlier. "No, I haven't seen any flyers."

Vicky informed her about the significant reward being offered for information. "They have a $50,000 reward for whoever may have seen something and can lead them to the person responsible for Scooby's death."

Suzzette felt slightly disconnected from her surroundings, realizing she must have missed the flyers. "I must have been in a haze this morning because I didn't see any flyers posted anywhere."

Vicky encouraged Suzzette to join the community's efforts to support Emily's family. "Yeah, they're posted everywhere, and you can't miss them. I pray they find the person who did this horrific act. Well, would you like to come along later after school? All the teachers are going by Emily's house to take some food and gifts to the house."

Suzzette agreed to join, expressing her willingness to help. "Sure, I would love to come along. I'm not doing much after work. I'll stop at the store and pick up a few items."

Vicky appreciated Suzzette's willingness to participate in the community's efforts. "Great, it's so good to see the community finally coming together in a very long time. And rallying around the family to show support. It's a shame that it takes a tragedy to bring people together."

Suzzette nodded, sharing her perspective on the division that had affected the community. "Yeah, I know. Since that last presidential election, everyone has been mad at each other. Some still haven't forgiven each other and are still not speaking to one another because of their opposing views."

Vicky sympathized with Suzzette's experience. "Oh, I know that all too well. Cindy and Dan haven't spoken to me or Paul after they found out we voted Republican. Isn't that unbelievable? We tried reaching out to them, but they wouldn't respond."

Suzzette expressed her frustration at the lack of forgiveness among Christians. "I thought they both were Christians. We all know that's not the way Christians should act. That makes people like me stay far from church."

Vicky encouraged her friend not to let such experiences deter her from attending church. "Well, you shouldn't let that keep you from going to church. God wants you to get to know him. He loves you, and he especially loves it when we fellowship together with one another at church."

Suzzette remained uncertain but took Vicky's words to heart. Their conversation shifted to another topic as Vicky asked about Johnnie, Suzzette's son.

"When is Johnnie coming back home to visit?" Vicky inquired.

Suzzette's face displayed a mixture of emotions as she answered, "I don't think he's coming back home."

Vicky was surprised and concerned. "Why do you say that?"

Suzzette elaborated on the strained relationship between Johnnie and his father. "He doesn't want to have anything to do with John. He thinks he's too hard on him."

Vicky probed further. "So, do you think he's too hard on him?"

Suzzette didn't hesitate to share her perspective. "Yes, I do. When Johnnie was home, John just wouldn't cut that boy any slack. Johnnie got fed up and left, and I don't blame him. And I don't like the fact that he keeps lying to me about drinking again. I really think his job has got him so stressed that he has started back drinking."

Vicky suggested a potential solution. "Suzzette, John needs help. You have to try and get him some help. Jerry is renting some space at the church to have AA meetings. He meets every Tuesday night at 6 PM. I have his card."

As their conversation continued, the two friends contemplated the challenges they faced within their community and families while also discussing the importance of forgiveness, understanding, and support.

CHAPTER SEVEN

Shards of Desolation

John's car swerved recklessly down the dimly lit streets of Hawthorn, the rhythmic hum of the engine mixed with the muffled tunes of a country song playing on the radio. Empty whiskey bottles clinked in the passenger seat, a stark reminder of his troubled journey.

In his rearview mirror, John's bloodshot eyes flickered as he nervously scanned the road behind him. Guilt and anger were etched across his face. Each sip from the bottle intensified his swirling emotions.

"Where are you, Suzzette?" he mumbled through slurred speech.

His foot pressed harder on the gas pedal, propelling the car faster down the road. The dimly lit street lights cast eerie shadows, mirroring the turmoil within him.

Finally, John's car lurched into the driveway of their modest home. His unsteady hands fumbled with the keys before he managed to open the front door. The scent of alcohol lingered in his wake as he stumbled inside.

Furniture became obstacles in his disoriented path. A vase tumbled from a table, shattering on the floor, the sound of broken glass a stark reminder of the chaos he brought with him.

"Suzzette, where are you?" he cried out, his voice a discordant blend of anger and confusion. He knew he was spiraling out of control, but the whiskey was a temporary salve for his wounded soul.

The house seemed to respond with deafening silence as John continued his aimless search. He reached his son's room, his heavy breathing punctuating the stillness. His eyes landed on a framed picture on the nightstand—a snapshot from happier days.

In the photo, Suzzette, Johnnie, and himself beamed with genuine joy. Their smiles, forever captured in the frame, were a stark contrast to the man now standing in the dimly lit room.

"You left me, Suzzette...and took him away," John muttered with a venomous edge to his words. His voice trembled as he spoke, and with a surge of unbridled rage, he snatched the picture frame from the nightstand.

The glass shattered upon impact with the wall, and the image of their once-happy family was obliterated into countless fragments that scattered across the room.

The house bore witness to this act of emotional devastation, the broken pieces of their past lying strewn across the floor like a metaphor for John's shattered life.

CHAPTER EIGHT

A Community Warm Embrace

The Stephenson residence was filled with warmth and empathy as teachers, friends, and their pastor gathered to support the grieving family. Tables were adorned with an array of food and gifts, a tangible expression of their love and concern for the Stephenson family.

Suzzette sat among her fellow teachers, engaged in conversations that bridged the gap between old friends and new acquaintances. As she exchanged smiles and stories, Vicky, Paul, and Suzzette stood together, sharing in the collective effort to bring solace to Emily's household.

Paul's familiar face brought a sense of nostalgia to Suzzette. He embraced her warmly, and as they exchanged a hug, he inquired about her family's well-being.

"How are you doing, Suzzette? Long time no see," Paul remarked, his eyes filled with genuine care.

Suzzette returned the hug with a grateful smile. "I'm doing great, thanks for asking."

Concern etched on his face, Paul continued, "How's John and Johnnie boy doing?"

Suzzette's gaze shifted to Vicky for a moment before she replied, "They're great. If you can say a little prayer for them both, that would be great."

Paul nodded, assuring her, "Sure."

Expressing her gratitude, Suzzette replied, "Thank you."

Their conversation was momentarily interrupted as Pastor Chad joined them, patting Paul on the back with a warm greeting. Handshakes and pleasantries were exchanged, reflecting the tight-knit community that had gathered in support.

"I'm doing great, Pastor. How about yourself?" Paul inquired.

"I'm blessed," Pastor Chad replied. He turned to Vicky, asking, "How are you doing, Vicky?"

Vicky's response was filled with positivity. "I'm doing well, thanks for asking."

With curiosity, Pastor Chad inquired about Suzzette, who was a newcomer to their community. "Who is this, may I ask? I haven't seen her at church."

Vicky introduced Suzzette warmly. "This is my friend Suzzette. She and her husband moved from New Jersey several months ago. I helped her get a position with me at

Stansbury Elementary. She teaches 2nd grade, and her husband John took a position in the Mayor's Office."

Pastor Chad, extending a hand, greeted Suzzette. "Pleased to meet you."

Suzzette reciprocated with a friendly smile. "Pleased to meet you as well."

With introductions complete, Pastor Chad excused himself, promising to catch up with them later. He walked away, his presence radiating comfort and reassurance.

Cindy and Dan arrived at the gathering, their arms laden with gifts and food. Emily's mother greeted them at the door with a warm embrace, and they handed their offerings over with heartfelt condolences.

Meanwhile, upstairs in Emily's bedroom, her mother checked in on her. Emily sat by the window, her gaze fixed on the changing leaves outside.

"Honey, are you hungry?" her mother inquired gently.

Emily shook her head, her voice soft. "No, I'm not hungry, Mom."

Concerned for her daughter, her mother moved closer. "What are you looking at out the window?"

They both peered outside, taking in the autumn scenery. "The leaves are beautiful, aren't they? Fall is certainly here."

Her mother enveloped Emily in a loving embrace, understanding the depth of her sorrow. "I know you miss Scooby. Your Dad and I both miss him too. Honey, you do know that you are going to have to eat something. Sis. Cindy brought you your favorite dish, the one you also asked her to make for you. Homemade lasagna, just the way you like it."

Emily's voice quivered as she responded, "I'm just not hungry right now. Where's Dad?"

Her mother reassured her, "Your father had to work a little late today. He should be home shortly. I won't pressure you to come downstairs. If you need something, just let me know."

Tears welled up in Emily's eyes, and she confided in her mother, "I really miss Scooby, Mom."

Her mother reached for a tissue, offering her comfort and understanding. "I know you do, honey. Let me get you some Kleenex."

As Emily's mother wiped away her tears, Pastor Chad addressed the community downstairs, their collective support and empathy serving as a reminder that they were not alone in their grief.

Pastor Chad stood before the gathered community, his words resonating with warmth and sincerity. The Stephenson residence had become a hub of support, a testament to the strength of their bonds in the face of tragedy. Tables adorned with food and gifts were a tangible expression of love and concern for the grieving family.

The mother, having come downstairs, stood in the back, her eyes filled with gratitude as she listened to Pastor Chad's heartfelt words. He spoke of unity, of setting aside differences, and of striving for peace in all aspects of life.

"If you all can gather together, join hands with one another for prayer," Pastor Chad requested, prompting hesitant glances among the attendees. It was as if they were unsure about this display of unity, but they soon overcame their reservations and joined hands.

As Pastor Chad continued, his voice filled with conviction and faith, the room became a sacred space where hearts came together in prayer. He invoked God's presence, drawing strength from the promise that when two or more gathered in His name, He would be in their midst.

"Father, as we all come together during this tragic time," Pastor Chad prayed, "you said in your word that whenever two or more are gathered in your name, there you will be in the midst." His words carried a soothing cadence, calming the hearts of those in the room.

He continued to pray for unity among mothers and daughters, fathers and sons, friends and families, communities, neighbors, and even politicians. He implored everyone to have a heart of forgiveness and to build the bonds that God intended for them. His prayer was a plea for the community to become a beacon of light, leading the world to God's love.

"Let our community be the light that leads the world to you," Pastor Chad said. "God, teach us to be good role models to the people around us and around the world so that when they see you and your love within us, they would want to know you more and more."

The room echoed with the collective "Amen" that followed, sealing their commitment to these heartfelt petitions. The pastor's words resonated deeply, touching the hearts of all present.

With the community now united in prayer, Pastor Chad addressed the urgent matter at hand—the search for the person responsible for Scooby's death. He called for vigilance, for every member to keep a watchful eye and report anything suspicious to the police. The tragic loss of Scooby was a stark reminder that their actions could prevent harm to others.

"Let's work together as a people, under one God who is in control of all things," Pastor Chad declared, his voice unwavering. "We need to find the person responsible for Scooby's death."

The room was filled with embraces and comforting gestures as the gathering concluded. Cindy and Dan shared heartfelt hugs with Paul and Vicky, their bonds strengthened through shared sorrow and a renewed sense of community.

Pastor Chad, meanwhile, approached Emily's mother, who had been standing in the background. Concern etched her face as she discussed Emily's well-being.

"How's she doing?" Pastor Chad inquired gently.

"She's not eating," Emily's mother replied with a sigh. "I'm trying to get her to eat."

Pastor Chad offered his support and a path to healing. "She's going to come around soon. I have some available counseling spots opened tomorrow at 1 pm. Bring her to the church. She is really going to need some therapy."

Gratitude filled Emily's mother's eyes as she accepted the offer. "Thanks, Pastor. I will bring her by tomorrow. I pulled her out of school for a couple of weeks so she can get some rest."

"Okay, I'll see you guys tomorrow," Pastor Chad said reassuringly. "Tell Matthew I'll call him later."

With that, Emily's mother nodded, her heart lighter with the knowledge that they had the support of their community and their pastor during this difficult time.

CHAPTER NINE

The Confrontation

Suzzette pulled her car into the driveway, exhaustion etched across her face after an emotionally taxing day. She stepped out of the car and made her way into the house, seeking solace in the comfort of her home. Little did she know, her own battles awaited her within those familiar walls.

Inside the kitchen, John was standing, his expression tense and frustrated. As Suzzette entered, his sudden presence caught her off guard, sending a jolt of surprise through her.

"Ooh, you scared me, John," Suzzette admitted with a nervous laugh.

But there was no hint of amusement in John's demeanor. He was upset, and his voice reflected it as he confronted her about her whereabouts.

"Where have you been all afternoon?" he questioned, his voice laced with frustration. "I've been calling you. Why didn't you pick up your phone?"

Suzzette sighed, her own patience beginning to wear thin. "I was at Stephenson's house."

"Why were you at their house? Did they have a party that I wasn't aware of?" John's tone grew more accusatory.

Suzzette, feeling the tension escalating, tried to explain. "It wasn't a party."

But John wasn't satisfied with her vague response. His voice raised as he demanded an answer, "Then what was it, Suzzette?"

The argument continued, and John's frustration became more apparent. He admitted to drinking, revealing a truth that had caused a rift between them before.

Suzzette, concerned for her husband's well-being and the impact of his drinking on their family, reached into her purse. She retrieved a card given to her by Vicky, a lifeline that could potentially lead John toward recovery.

"Vicky gave me a card for a guy down at the church who teaches an AA meeting every Tuesday night," Suzzette explained as she handed the card to John. Her voice was filled with compassion, but John's response was far from what she had hoped for.

He dismissed the idea with anger, tossing the card to the floor. "Well, I'm not going to no stupid AA meeting because I'm not an alcoholic!"

Suzzette, overwhelmed and disheartened by the encounter, decided to step away from the confrontation. "I'm going to pray for you, John," she said softly, her eyes glistening with unshed tears.

As she turned and left the room, John couldn't resist making one last hurtful remark. "Pray for me, huh? What about praying for yourself? How about that!"

Suzzette retreated to the bathroom, where her tears finally flowed freely. She needed a moment of solitude to collect herself and find the strength to face the challenges that lay ahead.

As she was lost in her thoughts, her cell phone rang, pulling her back into the present. It was her son, Johnnie, on the line.

"Hey, Johnnie," Suzzette greeted her son, her voice still trembling from the emotional encounter with her husband.

"Hey, Mom," Johnnie replied. "Dad made you cry again, didn't he?"

Suzzette sniffed, trying to compose herself. "I'm okay, Johnnie. You know how your Father gets when he's stressed."

Johnnie, concerned for his mother's well-being, couldn't help but express his frustration. "Mom, how long will you continue to make excuses for Dad? He can't keep treating you the way he does. It's not okay, that's one reason why I left, and I vowed to never come back as long as he's there."

Suzzette, torn between her love for her husband and her concern for her son, tried to offer a perspective of forgiveness and understanding. "Honey, you can't keep holding grudges against your Father. You have to learn to forgive."

Johnnie's voice was resolute as he responded, "I understand, Mother, but he has to learn how to treat people with respect. I love you,

Mother, but until Dad gets some help from all that drinking, I will not be stepping a foot in that house. Well, Mother, I have to go now. I love you, I'll talk to you soon."

Suzzette hung up the phone, her heart heavy with the weight of their family's struggles. She glanced at herself in the mirror, her reflection mirroring the emotional turmoil within her. She splashed water on her face, trying to wash away the pain and frustration of the day, knowing that she needed to find the strength to continue supporting her family, even in the face of adversity.

CHAPTER TEN

A Glimpse of Peace

The evening settled over Emily's house, enveloping it in a gentle calm. The father, Matthew, stood in the dimly lit hallway, his concern etched on his face. He couldn't resist the urge to check on Emily, his precious daughter, as she lay sound asleep in her room. With the utmost care, he pushed the door open, just enough to peer inside. Moonlight streamed through the curtains, casting a soft glow on Emily's peaceful form. Her chest rose and fell in a rhythmic pattern, a sight that eased Matthew's worried heart.

Satisfied that his daughter was resting comfortably, Matthew quietly retreated from her room and made his way to the master bedroom. There, he found his wife, Sarah, already in bed, her expression a mix of exhaustion and relief. Matthew began to remove his shoes and unbutton his shirt before joining her on the bed.

I see she's sleeping well. How long has she been asleep?

Sarah's voice barely rose above a whisper as she responded, her weariness evident.

She's been asleep for a while now. After everyone left, she took a bath, and I finally managed to get her to eat something. That's the best news I've heard all day. He reached out, intertwining his fingers with Kathy's, silently acknowledging the emotional weight they both carried. Pastor Chad mentioned that he'll call you later. He wants me to bring Emily to the church tomorrow for a counseling session at 1 PM. I think that's a wise decision.

CHAPTER ELEVEN

The Dog Named King

In the charming town of Willowbrook, nestled amidst rolling hills and peaceful meadows, there lived a kind-hearted pastor named Chad. With a warm smile and a heart full of compassion, he was a beloved figure in the community. His church, a quaint white building with a tall steeple, welcomed all who sought solace and guidance.

One sunny afternoon, a mother and her young daughter, Emily, arrived at Pastor Chad's office for a counseling session. Emily, a bright-eyed and curious child, was eager to share her thoughts and feelings with the wise pastor. Little did they know that this visit would not only offer guidance but also bring laughter and a deep bond between them.

As they settled into the cozy office, Pastor Chad decided to share a piece of his own childhood with Emily.

"You know what, Emily? I had a dog when I was your age," he began, a hint of nostalgia in his voice.

Emily's eyes widened with excitement. "You did, Pastor? What was his name?"

The pastor exchanged a knowing look with Emily's mother before replying, "His name was King, and boy do I miss King."

Emily leaned forward, eager to hear more. "What happened to King?" she asked.

Pastor Chad's expression turned solemn as he recounted a painful memory. "My stepfather didn't like King," he explained, his voice tinged with regret. He threatened us that if King chewed his shoes again, he would get rid of him for good. My sisters and I thought he was joking. We didn't think he would do something so mean. Boy, were we wrong."

Emily listened intently as Pastor Chad continued, sharing the heart-wrenching day from his childhood.

"When we came home from school, usually King would meet us at the door and jump all over us. But on that particular day, there was no King at the door. My sister and I frantically searched the house, and he was not there. Mother said, 'Tom got rid of King.' I tell you, Emily, that was the worst day of my life. It felt like someone ripped my heart out of my chest. I couldn't face my stepfather for weeks. Just the thought of what he did to King made me very angry."

Emily's eyes welled up with empathy as she listened to Pastor Chad's painful story. Her mother, too, was deeply moved by his vulnerability.

"But," Pastor Chad continued, "I knew at 7 years old that even though it hurt so bad, I had to forgive him. I had questions for God, just like you might have questions too. My question was if God is good and loving, why does he allow evil and suffering to exist? I remember my mother sitting me down and reading John 16:33, 'You will have suffering in this world.' I understood that at 7 years old. God didn't say you might - he said it is going to happen."

Emily nodded, absorbing the wisdom in Pastor Chad's words. She wiped away a tear and asked, "You might be asking why God allowed this to happen to Scooby?" The only honest answer I can give you is I don't know. I cannot stand in the shoes of God and give a complete answer to that question. I don't have God's mind. I don't see with God's eyes. So when you ask about why this happened to Scooby, you may not get the full answer in this world. Someday you'll see with clarity, but for now, things are foggy. We can't understand everything from our finite perspective. If they ever find the person who did this to Scooby, or if they never do, you have to make up your mind that you will forgive that person because that is what God would want us to do, okay?"

Emily nodded once more, her heart touched by Pastor Chad's words. "Okay, Pastor."

With their counseling session now over, Emily and her mother waved goodbye to Pastor Chad, their hearts a little lighter, and their spirits uplifted. They left his office with a newfound understanding of forgiveness and a deeper connection to their compassionate pastor, who had shared a piece of his own life to help them navigate the challenges of theirs.

Little did they know that their meetings with Pastor Chad would become a cherished part of their lives, filled not only with profound lessons but also with laughter and shared stories that would shape their bond forever.

CHAPTER TWELVE

The Journey of Hope

In the quietude of his kitchen, John's troubled eyes settled on the card for the upcoming Alcoholics Anonymous (AA) meeting. With a deep breath, he picked it up, his fingers trembling slightly as he studied the words printed on it. After a moment's contemplation, he tucked it carefully into his pocket and made his way to the door. Today was a new chapter in his life, a journey to face his demons head-on. As he slid into his car and started the engine, determination coursed through his veins, propelling him toward the meeting that held the promise of redemption.

While John embarked on his path to recovery, Suzzette, his partner, pulled up to their home. Concern etched across her face as she stepped out of the car and entered the familiar surroundings. The mail on the table drew her attention, but her thoughts were consumed by one question.

"John, are you home?" Suzzette called out, her voice a blend of worry and hope, echoing through the empty rooms.

She began her search, moving through each room with growing apprehension. It was in Johnnie's room that she stumbled upon a heartbreaking scene. A shattered picture frame lay on the floor, its contents scattered around it. Suzzette knelt to pick up the broken pieces and gazed at the photo that had once filled the frame.

"What happened?" she whispered to the absent John, her voice quivering with emotion. As she held the cherished image in her hands, she couldn't help but let her true feelings pour out.

"Mommie misses you so much, John John. Please come home soon."

CHAPTER THIRTEEN

Journey to Healing

As John continued on his journey, driving towards the AA meeting, he observed the world around him. The community seemed to be in motion, united in purpose. Families walked together, neighbors lent a helping hand, and the spirit of togetherness was palpable.

The community was not just coming together for companionship; they were determined to find the person responsible for Scooby's tragic fate. They knocked on doors, held each other in prayer, and showed unwavering solidarity in their quest for justice.

Amidst this unity, John arrived at the church hosting the AA meeting. Inside, a group of individuals sat in a circle, each person bearing their own burdens and seeking solace in the shared struggle. Jerry, the AA facilitator, occupied a chair in the center, clutching a box of tissues, ready to guide the participants through their journey of recovery.

Inside the modest meeting room at the local church, a group of individuals gathered for their regular Alcoholics Anonymous (AA) meeting. Jerry, the AA facilitator, sat in the center, holding a box of tissues, ready to guide the participants through their journey of recovery.

With an air of welcoming warmth, Jerry spoke to the room, "Are there any newcomers or first-timers attending the meeting who would like to introduce themselves?"

A sense of hope and anticipation filled the air as Lucas, a participant seeking solace in the group, raised his hand eagerly.

"Go ahead, Lucas," encouraged Jerry.

With a hint of nervousness, Lucas introduced himself, his voice steady and determined, "My name is Lucas, and today is my first day here."

The room erupted in applause, a symphony of support and encouragement that enveloped Lucas in a reassuring embrace.

Jerry smiled and continued, "Let's welcome Lucas with a round of applause, everyone."

The group's applause was not merely polite; it was a genuine celebration of Lucas's courage and a promise of solidarity.

"We're glad to have you here, Lucas," Jerry added, his words carrying the weight of the group's collective empathy.

Lucas nodded in acknowledgment, feeling the warmth of acceptance wash over him. It was a pivotal moment in his journey towards recovery, finding a community that understood and welcomed him without judgment.

As the meeting continued, another figure made his entrance, quietly slipping into the room. John, his face etched with uncertainty and vulnerability, captured the attention of the group with curious glances.

Jerry, the ever-attentive facilitator, noticed John's arrival and offered a gentle greeting, "Hello, sir. How may I help you?"

John hesitated for a moment, his inner turmoil evident. He finally spoke, his voice tinged with a mix of desperation and hope, "I was told this is where you meet for the AA meeting. Am I in the right place? Or should I leave?"

Jerry's response was filled with understanding and compassion, "Oh no, you don't have to leave. You are in the right place. Come on over and grab a seat."

John scanned the room, his apprehension palpable. Each seat held a story of struggle, a journey toward healing, and a battle against addiction. Eventually, he mustered the strength to overcome his hesitation and made his way over to a vacant seat. As he settled in, the weight of his past choices bore down on his shoulders.

Jerry encouraged him one more time, "Can you introduce yourself to the class?"

John, his gaze fixed on the floor for a moment, summoned the courage to speak his truth, "My name is John, and thank you for having me."

In that simple introduction, John took the first step on his own path to recovery, surrounded by a room filled with people who understood his journey, each one offering their support and understanding. The room buzzed with a shared sense of purpose and hope as the meeting continued, binding these individuals together in their pursuit of healing and redemption.

John looked around the room filled with expectant faces, each person carrying their own burdens and seeking solace within the circle of Alcoholics Anonymous. As he made his way over to an empty seat, the uncertainty in his eyes was palpable.

Jerry, the group's compassionate facilitator, welcomed John with a reassuring smile, "We're glad to have you, John."

Before delving into the personal stories that would soon unfold, Jerry began by leading the group in a collective recitation of the Serenity Prayer. The words of the prayer hung in the air, offering a moment of reflection and unity.

"God, grant me the serenity To accept the things I cannot change; Courage to change the things I can; and wisdom to know the difference."

With the serenity prayer serving as a grounding force, Jerry proceeded to explain the AA Preamble, emphasizing the fellowship's core principles and purpose. He stressed that Alcoholics Anonymous was a place where individuals shared their experiences, strengths, and hopes to collectively address the common problem of alcoholism. Membership required only the desire to stop drinking, with no financial obligations. Jerry also emphasized that AA remained independent of external affiliations, politics, and causes, existing solely to help alcoholics achieve and maintain sobriety.

"Now," Jerry said, turning his attention to John, "since we are starting counterclockwise, I need you to tell us your story."

John glanced around the room, the weight of his past experiences etched on his face. Jerry's reassuring presence gave him the courage to continue.

"It's okay, John. You can go ahead," Jerry encouraged.

Taking a deep breath, John began, "Again, my name is John, and I'm an alcoholic." His voice quivered, and he hesitated briefly before opening up about the painful memories that had haunted him for years.

"I remember growing up, Dad was really harsh toward Mom and me," John recounted. His voice trembled as he shared the torment of his upbringing. "He would come into the house after having way too much to drink."

As John spoke, his audience listened attentively, understanding the catharsis that came with sharing one's darkest moments.

"Dad would yell at Mother for no reason," he continued. "He would slam her against the wall until she was almost unconscious. He would beat me until my backside bruised and bled. The next day he would apologize, and the vicious cycle went on day in and day out."

John's voice quivered further, and he wiped away tears as he revealed the painful details. "I couldn't cry out for help because he would threaten to kill Mother if I told a soul. I thought my father hated me for being born. This abuse went on all the way through high school."

As John shared the torment he had endured, the room seemed to hold its breath, as if bearing witness to his pain.

"I started drinking when I was in high school," John admitted, his voice heavy with regret. "I needed something to help me escape the madness. I remember the last confrontation I had with Dad. I was drinking heavily by this time, and my poor mother didn't know what to do with either of us."

John's words hung in the air, the weight of his experiences palpable in the room. Tears streamed down his face as he recounted the final, devastating incident. "We became monstrous in the house against each other. The last straw was when I hit Father, and I hurt him and caused him to be hospitalized."

The room was filled with a heavy silence as John's emotions overwhelmed him. Jerry offered him a box of Kleenex, and John accepted it gratefully, wiping away his tears.

"You can finish up next week," Jerry reassured him, recognizing the emotional toll of John's story.

With that, John took a moment to collect himself, knowing that this was just the beginning of his journey to healing and recovery, surrounded by a group that understood and supported him in ways he had never imagined. John's voice trembled as he continued to pour out his painful memories, his emotions raw and unfiltered. Tears streamed down his face as he bared his soul to the supportive circle of the Alcoholics Anonymous meeting.

"I didn't mean to," John cried, his voice choked with emotion. "I was only trying to help Mother. I just exploded!"

Jerry, the compassionate facilitator, reached over and handed John a Kleenex, offering a comforting gesture as a lifeline in his moment of vulnerability.

"Here you go, John," Jerry said softly, his eyes filled with empathy.

As John wiped away his tears and composed himself, Jerry gently reassured him, "You can finish up next week."

The room remained enveloped in a heavy silence, the weight of John's confession hanging in the air. The participants in the group understood the courage it took for him to share his darkest moments, and they offered him their unwavering support.

John knew that this was just the beginning of his journey to healing and redemption. He had taken the first crucial steps in confronting his past, acknowledging his struggle with alcoholism, and seeking solace and understanding among those who had walked a similar path. The tears he shed were not just tears of pain but also tears of hope, as he began to believe that recovery and transformation were possible.

As the meeting continued, John clung to the newfound sense of community he had discovered, a group of individuals who had opened their hearts to him without judgment. The road ahead would be challenging, but with the support of his fellow AA members and the guidance of Jerry, he felt a glimmer of optimism that he had not experienced in a long time.

In the weeks to come, John would delve deeper into his past, confront his addiction, and work toward mending the wounds that had haunted him for years. With each meeting, he would find strength in the shared stories of recovery and the unwavering support of his newfound family.

And so, in the quiet moments that followed John's emotional confession, the room echoed with the unspoken promise of redemption and the collective belief that, together, they could find the courage to change the things they could and the wisdom to know the difference.

CHAPTER FOURTEEN

The Search for Scooby's Justice

Inside Emily's cozy home, a sense of normalcy had settled in. The kitchen table was adorned with a carefully prepared meal, and the family sat together, passing dishes of food and sharing the warmth of togetherness.

Emily's mother couldn't contain her excitement as she shared the news, her face glowing with happiness. "Emily's counseling session with Pastor Chad went great!"

Emily's father chimed in with a smile, expressing his joy, "That's so good to hear, honey."

Emily, their young daughter, couldn't wait to share what she learned during her counseling session. She spoke with enthusiasm, her eyes sparkling. "Pastor Chad had a dog when he was my age."

Her father leaned in, eager to hear more. "Oh yeah?"

Emily nodded, her voice filled with wonder. "Yes, his name was King. His stepfather was very mean. He got rid of him while Pastor and his sister were at school, all because King chewed up his shoes. That really hurt Pastor. He thought he could never forgive him for doing that. But Pastor said he did forgive his stepfather for taking his dog away."

Her father nodded in agreement, offering his wisdom. "Honey, it's always good to forgive. That's what God wants us to do. The Bible says in Ephesians 4:32, 'Be kind and compassionate to one another, forgiving each other, just as in Christ God forgave us.'"

As the family enjoyed their meal and shared their stories, the phone suddenly rang, interrupting their conversation. Emily's father instinctively made a move to answer it, but her mother insisted on taking the call.

"I'll get it," her father offered, but her mother was already on her way to the phone.

"Hello," Emily's mother greeted the caller with a warm tone.

A voice on the other end identified itself as Officer Peterson. Emily's mother listened attentively as the officer spoke.

"Hi, Mrs. Stephenson, this is Officer Peterson," the voice on the phone said.

Emily's mother's tone shifted to concern. "Hi, Officer Peterson, is everything okay?"

Officer Peterson reassured her, "Everything is okay. We got a tip today. Someone called in and stated that they saw a blue Chevy pickup truck speeding really fast up the street the day Scooby was hit. They said that they have seen that same truck around in the neighborhood."

Emily's mother's eyes widened with interest. "Do you all know who the truck belongs to?"

Officer Peterson responded, "That we do not know yet."

Meanwhile, at the kitchen table, Emily's father and Emily herself sat in anticipation, their curiosity piqued. The search for answers had taken a step forward, and the hope of justice for Scooby burned brighter in their hearts than ever before.

Around the cozy kitchen table, the family had enjoyed a satisfying meal, the clinking of utensils and the warmth of shared moments creating an atmosphere of contentment.

"I am so full now," Emily exclaimed, patting her satisfied tummy.

Father Matthew couldn't resist teasing her, "What about dessert? Do you have any room for some homemade apple pie with whipped cream and vanilla ice cream?"

Emily chuckled, her voice filled with amusement, "I don't think I can put anything else in my tummy."

Father and Emily shared a laugh, their bond growing stronger with every moment spent together.

Meanwhile, Emily's mother had taken the call from Officer Peterson and was now joining the family at the table. She shared the details of the call with them.

"We're going to run this information into the system and see what we can come up with," Officer Peterson had informed her. "If anything comes back, we will let you know."

Emily's mother expressed her gratitude, "Okay, thanks for calling Officer Peterson. We appreciate all you guys' hard work down there at the precinct."

Officer Peterson replied with humility, "You don't have to thank us; this is our job. Have a great evening, Mrs. Stephenson."

"Thank you, you too," Emily's mother replied before hanging up.

Returning to the kitchen table, she found her husband and daughter digging into slices of apple pie.

"You guys couldn't wait on me," she observed with a playful smile.

Father Matthew playfully pointed a fork at Emily, pretending to accuse her. "Sorry, we couldn't wait on you. Emily made me do it."

Emily giggled, her eyes sparkling with mischief. "No, Daddy, you made me do it."

Laughter filled the room, a beautiful melody of family togetherness that dispelled any remaining tension.

Later that evening, as the day wound down, Emily's mother lovingly tucked her into bed.

"You're ready for school tomorrow," she remarked with a hint of pride.

Emily's eyes shone with excitement. "Yes, I am. I miss my friends, especially Cassey."

Her mother couldn't help but inquire, "What about your teachers?"

Emily, with her typical childlike innocence, responded with a mischievous smile, "What about them?"

The two of them shared a hearty laugh, savoring the precious moments of laughter and warmth that were at the heart of their family. With each passing day, their bond grew stronger, and the hope of justice for Scooby remained alive in their hearts, a testament to the power of love and togetherness.

In the quiet of Emily's bedroom, the mother couldn't help but ask, "Don't you miss them?"

Emily, tucked snugly beneath her covers, responded with youthful exasperation, "They give me too much homework."

Both mother and daughter burst into laughter, their shared moment of amusement a reminder of the simple joys of family life.

"Well, you better get some sleep so you can be rested for tomorrow," Emily's mother gently advised as she leaned over to kiss her daughter's forehead. She then turned off the bedside lamp, casting the room into a comforting darkness.

"Goodnight, honey," she whispered, her love and warmth palpable.

"I love you too, goodnight, Mom," Emily replied, her voice softening as she settled in for a peaceful night's sleep.

Leaving Emily's room, her mother descended the stairs to join her husband, who was engrossed in watching television.

"What was that call about earlier?" Father inquired, curious about the phone call he had overheard earlier.

Emily's mother settled into the sofa beside him, ready to share the news. "It was Officer Peterson from down at the precinct. I wanted to make sure Emily was asleep first before talking about it. He said they received a tip today. Someone called in and mentioned that they saw a blue Chevy pickup truck speeding up the street really fast the day Scooby got hit."

Father's eyes lit up with hope. "Really? That's good news, honey."

Emily's mother nodded with a sense of optimism. "Yes, it is. They're going to put that information in the system to see what they can come up with. You know the police have ways to find out everything. Let's believe that God is answering our prayers."

Father leaned closer, reflecting on the positive changes he had observed in their community. "I'm so glad to see our community coming together. It's bad what happened to Scooby, but I'm seeing so much good happening out of this."

Emily's mother couldn't agree more. "I know, thank God, it's been well overdue. Emily told me that she forgives the person who did this to Scooby. She said if she saw the person, she would hug them. I thought that was so awesome to hear her say that."

Father nodded in agreement, his thoughts turning to the lessons of forgiveness. "That's what forgiveness is all about. The Bible says in Ephesians 4:31-32, 'Get rid of all bitterness, rage, and anger, brawling and slander, along with every form of malice. Be kind and compassionate to one another, forgiving each other, just as in Christ God forgave you.'"

As they sat together in the soft glow of the television, their hearts filled with hope, Emily's parents knew that their family and their community were on a path toward healing and redemption. In the darkness of the night, the light of forgiveness and unity shone brightly, illuminating their journey forward.

CHAPTER FIFTEEN

The Search for Scooby's Justice

The days had turned into weeks, and the community's determination to find justice for Scooby burned brighter than ever. Emily's parents, along with their neighbors, continued their relentless quest to uncover the truth behind the hit-and-run that had shaken their peaceful neighborhood.

Emily's mother had spent countless hours with the police, providing any information that could lead to a breakthrough. She was determined to see the responsible party brought to justice for the sake of her family and the memory of Scooby.

Emily's Father Matthew had rallied his fellow community members, encouraging them to share any leads or suspicious sightings they might have. Their collective efforts were a testament to the strength of a tight-knit community determined to protect its own.

The tip about the blue Chevy pickup truck had rekindled hope, and the police were working diligently to trace the vehicle and its owner. The community remained on high alert, ready to support the investigation in any way possible.

Emily, too, had been an inspiration. Her unwavering forgiveness and kindness had touched the hearts of those around her. She had become a symbol of compassion and love, even in the face of adversity. The way she had spoken of forgiving the person responsible for Scooby's death had resonated deeply with everyone who heard her story.

As the investigation continued, the community meetings became a hub of information and support. The bond among the neighbors grew stronger with each passing day, a testament to the power of unity in the face of tragedy.

In this chapter of their lives, Emily's family and their neighbors were not just searching for justice for Scooby; they were also rediscovering the strength that came from standing together in times of hardship. The search for justice had become a search for the enduring spirit of their community, a spirit that would not be broken, no matter the obstacles they faced.

CHAPTER SIXTEEN

Unveiling the Truth

John and Suzzette sat in their living room, a heavy silence hanging in the air. Suzzette had just delivered unsettling news about John's truck.

"Did they find the person?" John inquired, his voice tinged with hope.

Suzzette hesitated before responding, "No, but they do have some leads. There's also a $50,000 reward for whoever can help them find the person responsible."

John's face tightened with concern. "Well, I hope they find the person."

Suzzette studied John, her gaze filled with confusion and worry. His words seemed oddly detached from the situation.

"I'll be back. I need to go make a quick run," John announced abruptly, grabbing the truck keys and heading out the door.

He drove in silence, his thoughts weighing heavily on him. John's destination was the church, a place he hoped would provide him with some clarity.

Inside the church, Pastor Chad was packing up his belongings, preparing to leave for the night. John entered quietly, his demeanor one of a man wrestling with internal turmoil.

"Sir, may I help you?" Pastor Chad inquired, noticing the unease in John's presence.

John hesitated for a moment, then spoke, "I was looking for Jerry."

Pastor Chad shook his head gently. "Oh, Jerry's not here today. Jerry is here only on Tuesday evenings; he teaches an AA meeting."

John nodded in acknowledgment. "Yeah, I know. I'm a part of the group. I just needed someone to talk to before Tuesday. Thanks for your time; I'll go now."

As John turned to leave, Pastor Chad called out, "Sir, I'm available to talk."

John paused, his footsteps halting. He looked back at the pastor, his eyes filled with a mixture of uncertainty and a longing for guidance.

Meanwhile, Suzzette had called Vicky, a close friend, to share her concerns about John's truck.

"Hello?" Vicky answered.

Suzzette took a deep breath before explaining, "Do you have a minute to talk?"

Vicky, sensing the urgency in Suzzette's tone, replied, "Yes, what's wrong?"

Suzzette hesitated briefly before revealing, "There's a dent on the passenger side of John's truck."

Vicky was taken aback. "What do you mean there's a dent on the passenger's side of John's truck?"

Suzzette's voice trembled as she continued, "Remember you said that the police got a tip that someone saw a blue Chevy pickup truck speeding up the street the day Scooby got hit, and that there should be a dent on the passenger's side?"

A heavy silence hung between them as Vicky processed the implications. Finally, she asked, "What are you trying to say, Suzzette? That John hit Scooby?"

Suzzette's voice wavered as she replied, "I don't know. All I'm saying is there's a dent on the passenger's side of John's truck, and it was not there before."

Vicky's voice held a sense of urgency, "So what are you going to do?"

Suzzette's distress was palpable. "I don't know."

Vicky implored her friend, "You can't keep quiet about this, Suzzette, or you become an accessory to the crime. You're going to have to say something."

Suzzette's anxiety deepened as she considered the consequences. "How am I going to do that and risk John losing his job? John just got a major promotion, working alongside Mayor Thompson. If they find out about this, he could very well lose that position."

Vicky's tone grew stern as she reminded her friend, "I can't believe what I'm hearing, Suzzette. It's not about John or you. It's about doing what's right. Emily lost Scooby in the process. Was he drinking again?"

Suzzette's voice quivered as she admitted, "I don't know. He very well could have been."

As the phone call with Vicky came to an abrupt end, Suzzette was left in stunned silence. She stared at her phone, feeling the heavy weight of her moral dilemma pressing down on her. Vicky's stern words lingered in her ears, like a harsh and necessary wake-up call.

"I'm hoping you do the right thing, Suzzette. I can't sit on this phone any longer," Vicky had said before hanging up. Her voice had been filled with a mix of concern and frustration, leaving Suzzette in a state of turmoil.

Suzzette knew that she couldn't ignore the truth any longer. She had witnessed something that implicated her husband, John, in a terrible crime, and her silence was beginning to eat away at her conscience. She had a choice to make, one that would have profound consequences for her family, her husband's career, and her own sense of morality.

Tears welled up in Suzzette's eyes as she grappled with the decision before her. She knew that doing the right thing might mean revealing a painful truth and facing the consequences head-on. But she also understood that keeping silent could make her complicit in a terrible injustice.

The room around her seemed to close in, and the weight of her decision bore heavily on her shoulders. She needed to find the strength to confront the truth, to seek justice for Scooby, and to do what was right, even if it meant facing the unimaginable consequences.

In the darkness of her living room, Suzzette made a silent promise to herself and to her son Johnnie. She knew that the path to redemption was paved with difficult choices, and it was time to find the courage to make them. The journey towards the light of truth had begun, and it was a path Suzzette was determined to walk, no matter how challenging it might be.

CHAPTER SEVENTEEN

A Sanctuary of Redemption

In the quiet solitude of the church, John's tears flowed freely as he poured out his heart to Pastor Chad. The weight of his actions, the guilt, and the overwhelming sense of despair had finally found a voice. He had come to the church seeking solace and guidance, knowing that he had reached a crossroads in his life where he could no longer deny the darkness within him.

Pastor Chad listened patiently, his reassuring presence providing a glimmer of hope in the midst of John's turmoil. With compassion in his voice, he reminded John that there was nothing too great for God to forgive, that God's love was boundless and unconditional. He cited the Bible, emphasizing God's love for humanity and His willingness to extend grace, even in the face of human imperfections.

As John openly confessed his shortcomings and struggles, he was met with understanding and empathy. The burden of self-condemnation began to lift, replaced by the possibility of redemption. The realization that he had the power to change his path, with God's guidance, stirred something deep within him.

Tears streamed down John's face, a mix of remorse and newfound hope. He yearned to be the father his son deserved, to rebuild the fractured relationships in his life, and to find peace within himself. Pastor Chad saw this transformation taking place before his eyes, and he knew that John was ready to take a significant step towards healing and forgiveness.

With unwavering faith, John accepted Pastor Chad's invitation to embrace Christ in his life. Together, they recited the sinner's prayer, a solemn declaration of surrender and a plea for salvation. In that sacred moment, John felt a profound shift within himself, a glimmer of the light that had eluded him for so long.

"Thank you so much," John whispered, his voice filled with gratitude and a newfound sense of purpose. He knew that his journey towards redemption was just beginning, but he was no longer alone. With God's love and guidance, he had taken the first step on the path to a new beginning.

The church's silent sanctity enveloped them, offering solace and the promise of transformation. John's tears now carried a different weight—not of despair, but of hope, redemption, and the promise of a brighter future.

John left the church with a new look on life, as he was driving raindrops cascaded down the windshield of John's pickup truck, blurring his vision as he navigated the slick, winding roads. Thoughts of his recent conversation with Pastor Chad lingered in his mind. He had taken the first step towards redemption, seeking solace and forgiveness in the embrace of faith. Little did he know that the path to redemption would take an unexpected turn, one that would test his newfound resolve.

As he drove through the storm, each raindrop seemed to carry the weight of his past mistakes. The world outside blurred into a watery canvas, matching the turbulence within his heart. John's grip on the steering wheel tightened as he wrestled with his inner demons.

Suddenly, a car veered recklessly into his lane, its headlights blinding him for a moment. Panic surged through him as he swerved to avoid the impending collision. Time seemed to slow down, and the world turned surreal as the two vehicles collided with a deafening crash.

The impact was jarring, and the airbags deployed with a violent burst. Bystanders, alerted by the cacophony of metal meeting metal, rushed toward the scene. Sirens wailed in the distance, heralding the arrival of ambulances and police cars.

In the midst of chaos, John was trapped in his mangled truck, disoriented and in pain. Blood trickled from a gash on his forehead, his vision blurred. Concerned voices and hurried footsteps surrounded him, but their words were a distant echo.

Meanwhile, Suzzette, at home and oblivious to the unfolding tragedy, received an unexpected call. Her hand trembled as she answered, and the words from the other end of the line sent shockwaves through her.

"Your husband has been in a car accident. We need you at the hospital," said the voice on the phone.

Suzzette's heart raced as she grabbed her purse and car keys, leaving everything behind in her haste. Fear and confusion etched across her face as she hurriedly made her way to the hospital, praying for John's safety.

In another part of town, their son Johnnie received the same dreaded news. His heart pounded as he ran out of the house, his only thought was to reach his father's side.

Back at the accident scene, the paramedics worked urgently to extract John from the wreckage. His world spun in a daze as he was placed on a gurney and wheeled towards the waiting ambulance. Time hung suspended in that moment, his past and present colliding with devastating force.

As John was rushed to the hospital, his family raced to his side, their lives forever altered by the collision of fate. In that fateful instant, the promise of redemption was put to the test, and the uncertain road ahead would challenge their faith, their strength, and their love.

In the dimly lit hospital room, the steady hum of medical equipment was a stark contrast to the chaos that had unfolded just moments ago. John lay in the hospital bed, his face bandaged, connected to machines that monitored his every breath. Suzzette and Johnnie stood on either side of the bed, their hearts heavy with worry and fear.

Suzzette, her eyes swollen from crying, reached out and gently clasped John's hand. It was a feeble attempt to convey her love, her desperation, and her unyielding hope for his recovery.

"John," she whispered, her voice trembling with emotion, "I love you, and Johnnie loves you too." She looked at her son, his eyes filled with concern, and knew that they were in this together, no matter what lay ahead.

Johnnie, with his youthful determination, stood steadfast by his father's side. His unwavering belief in his dad's strength had always been a source of inspiration. He knew that they faced a daunting journey, but he refused to let despair take hold.

The doctor, a reassuring figure in the midst of their turmoil, had delivered both good and concerning news. John's stability was a relief, but the induced coma and swelling on his brain remained a looming threat. The uncertainty of what the future held weighed heavily on Suzzette's heart.

As they gazed upon John's motionless form, memories flooded their minds—of happier times, of the moments that defined their family, and of the hope that had carried them through life's trials.

Suzzette leaned down and kissed John's forehead, her tears falling onto his bandages. "Please, John," she whispered, "come back to us. We need you."

Johnnie added his voice, his voice filled with determination, "Dad, we're not giving up on you. We'll be right here when you wake up."

In that silent hospital room, surrounded by the beeping of machines and the quiet determination of a family united in love, there was a glimpse of hope—a belief that even in the face of adversity, they could find the strength to overcome.

The future remains uncertain, but as they stood together by John's side, they were reminded that love and hope had the power to conquer even the darkest of moments.

Suzzette sat in the hospital waiting room, her head buried in her lap, tears streaming down her face. The weight of worry and fear pressed heavily on her chest. Her husband, John, had left their home earlier with a hurried promise that he had to make a quick run. But hours had passed, and there was no word from him, only a growing sense of dread.

Suddenly, Suzzette felt a gentle tap on her shoulder. She looked up to see her son, Johnnie, standing there. Without a word, they embraced tightly, tears mingling with their relief at being together.

Suzzette's voice trembled as she spoke, "I don't understand what happened. He left and said he had to make a run."

Johnnie held his mother even closer, offering the reassurance that he desperately wished he felt. "Everything's going to be okay, Mom."

Suzzette continued to cry, her head resting on Johnnie's shoulder. Just then, a doctor approached them.

Suzzette, her worry etched on her face, asked, "Doctor, how's my husband? Is everything okay?"

The doctor introduced himself as Doctor Jacob, extending a handshake to both Suzzette and Johnnie. "He's doing just fine,

Mrs. Steinburg. I'm Doctor Jacob; it's a pleasure to meet you. The good news is that he's stable now."

Relief washed over Suzzette, but the doctor's next words cast a shadow over her hopes. "However, we had to put him into an induced coma because of the swelling on his brain. We were able to stop the bleeding, but the swelling is a concern for us, so we need to keep a very close watch on him."

Suzzette's heart sank, and she exchanged a worried glance with Johnnie.

"Are we able to see him?" Suzzette asked, her voice filled with urgency.

"Sure," replied Doctor Jacob.

Suzzette and Johnnie followed the doctor into John's room. Tubes and wires surrounded his motionless form, and his head was wrapped in bandages. Suzzette reached out and gently held her husband's hand, her tears falling onto the hospital sheets.

"John, I love you," Suzzette whispered, her voice quivering, "and Johnnie loves you too. You're strong, and we know you will come out of this. We need you, honey."

Suzzette continued to cry, her emotions pouring out as she clung to her husband's hand. After a moment, she left the room, needing a moment of solitude to gather her thoughts.

Johnnie stood on the other side of the bed, looking down at his father. He leaned in and kissed John's forehead.

"I love you, pops," Johnnie said softly. Then, he looked up toward the heavens and began to sob.

"God, if you can hear me," Johnnie's voice quivered with emotion, "please forgive me for ignoring you all those times you told me to forgive my father. I was so angry with him, and I felt like he didn't deserve to be forgiven for how he treated me and mother. But God, you know what's best, even when we don't know. I vow to listen to you when you speak. Please forgive me. I also forgive my father for hurting my mother, and in the way he did. If we ever needed you, it's right now."

CHAPTER EIGHTEEN

Unspoken Guilt and Divine Intervention

Inside Vicky and Paul's House. Paul called out to his wife from the living room. "Honey, are you ready? Pastor Chad will be here in a minute, so we can get up to the hospital."

Vicky, Paul's wife, yelled down from upstairs, "I'm coming now."

She quickly descended the stairs, her face a mix of concern and compassion. The news of John's accident had sent shockwaves through the family, and they were all rallying around Suzzette and Johnnie in their time of need.

As Vicky descended the stairs, Paul's somber voice broke the silence in the room.

"You know that we're going to have to report John to the police. He fits the description of the driver who killed Scooby," Paul remarked, his expression filled with a mix of concern and resolve.

Vicky locked eyes with her husband, her thoughts racing as she considered the gravity of the situation. "Yeah, I know. I wanted Suzzette to report it."

Paul nodded in agreement, acknowledging Suzzette's reluctance. "Honey, you know she's not going to do that."

Vicky sighed, a heavy weight on her heart. "I think she will."

Paul shook his head in disbelief. "Unbelievable."

Vicky proposed an alternative plan. "Let's first talk with Pastor and see what he thinks would be a good approach to this."

Just then, the car horn outside blared, signaling the arrival of Pastor Chad. Vicky grabbed her purse, and she and Paul headed out to the car. Pastor Chad took the wheel, and they began their journey to the hospital.

"Good morning," Pastor Chad greeted as they settled into the car.

"Good morning, Pastor," Vicky and Paul replied in unison.

Pastor Chad, sensing the tension in the car, inquired about when they had received the news about John.

Vicky explained, "Suzzette didn't tell me until this morning."

The pastor contemplated the timing and the events leading up to the accident. "It must have happened right after he left the church last night. He came by the church looking for Jerry. He's been coming out to the AA meeting Jerry teaches on Tuesday evenings. Jerry wasn't there, and something was troubling him, and he needed to talk. So we talked. Last night, I prayed with him, and we went over the salvation prayer together. He gave his life to Christ last night."

Paul couldn't contain his joy. "Praise God! Hallelujah."

Vicky echoed his sentiments. "That's the best news ever."

As the car continued down the road, Vicky raised a delicate issue. "Pastor, did he tell you that he killed Scooby?"

Pastor Chad was taken aback. "No, he didn't tell me that. How do you know it was him?"

Vicky provided the incriminating evidence. "There was a lead that had come into the police station that the vehicle that hit Scooby was a blue Chevy pickup truck. Given how hard Scooby was hit, that truck would have a huge dent on the front end of the passenger's side. Suzzette told me that she looked at the front end of the passenger's side of John's truck, and there was a huge dent with some blood on the truck."

Pastor Chad was perplexed. "Why didn't anyone say something?"

Vicky glanced at her husband, Paul, who decided to speak up. "Pastor, Vicky was going to report this, but she wanted Suzzette to report it, being that it's her husband. Suzzette was very much afraid to say anything. However, Vicky did convince her that she should report it."

As Pastor Chad's words reverberated through the car, the atmosphere grew tense, weighed down by the gravity of their impending decision. The hospital loomed in the distance, and their silence was broken only by the hum of the engine.

"Someone has to report this today," Pastor Chad's voice carried the undeniable urgency of the situation.

Vicky and Paul exchanged concerned glances, their hearts heavy with the knowledge of John's actions and the moral dilemma that now confronted them.

VICKY (Pensively) You're right, Pastor. We can't ignore this. It's a matter of justice, and it's the right thing to do.

Paul nodded solemnly, wrestling with the conflicting emotions within him. "But we also need to be there for Suzzette and Johnnie during this difficult time."

Pastor Chad, a man of unwavering faith and principles, acknowledged the complexities of the situation. "Of course, supporting them emotionally is essential, but we must ensure that justice prevails. We can't let fear or hesitation stop us from doing what's right."

The car pulled into the hospital parking lot, and an unspoken understanding hung in the air. They all knew that a crucial decision lay ahead, one that would shape the course of events in the coming days. The truth about John's involvement in Scooby's tragic accident had to come to light, and the path forward was uncertain. But guided by their moral compass and their commitment to truth and justice, they were prepared to face the challenges that lay ahead.

CHAPTER NINETEEN

Reunion Amidst Uncertainty

Inside the sterile, fluorescent-lit hospital corridors, the air was filled with the hurried steps of doctors and nurses. Pastor Chad, Paul, and Vicky entered the hospital, their hearts heavy with concern. They spotted Suzzette in the waiting area, and her eyes welled up with tears at the sight of her friends. Without hesitation, Vicky and Suzzette rushed towards each other, their embrace a comforting anchor amidst the chaos, as they shared a heartfelt hug.

Suzzette's tear-streaked face bore a fragile smile as she expressed her gratitude.

"Thanks for coming," she whispered, her voice quivering with emotion.

Vicky's response was filled with genuine affection as she reassured her friend.

"Anytime, honey. That's what friends are for."

Suzzette's eyes turned towards Pastor Chad and Paul, who greeted her with warm and reassuring hugs. Pastor Chad's concern was evident in his words.

"How's John doing?"

Suzzette's voice carried a glimmer of hope as she provided an update.

"He's still in an induced coma. The doctors are doing everything they can to reduce the swelling in his brain. The good news is they managed to stop the bleeding."

Pastor Chad offered a comforting nod, acknowledging the progress made. The group's concern remained palpable as they moved towards the next chapter of this uncertain journey.

Pastor Chad, Vicky, Paul, and Suzzette stood outside Johnnie's hospital room, their footsteps echoing through the sterile hallway. Emotions ran high as they prepared to step into the room where Johnnie lay.

Vicky, the vivacious and warm-hearted friend, couldn't contain her excitement. She pushed open the door and exclaimed, "Hey Johnnie boy, how are you? Long time no see."

Johnnie turned his head toward the door, his eyes lighting up with a mixture of surprise and joy. "Vicky," he said, his voice filled with warmth. "I'm doing great. How are you?"

Vicky stepped closer, enveloping Johnnie in a warm hug. "I'm blessed," she replied, her words infused with genuine happiness.

Paul, the ever-reliable and down-to-earth friend, followed suit. He extended his hand towards Johnnie and said, "Hey bud, how have you been?"

Johnnie grasped Paul's hand firmly. "I'm good," he replied with a smile.

"How's college life been treating you?" Paul asked, genuinely curious.

Johnnie leaned back into his pillows, reflecting on the past few months. "It's good," he admitted. "I can't complain. But I ain't even going to lie though. I miss my mom's home-cooked meals, especially those buttermilk biscuits."

Laughter filled the room as memories of Suzzette's delicious cooking flooded their minds.

Vicky chimed in, teasing Johnnie, "Boy, you don't look like you missed any meals. You picked up a little weight."

Johnnie chuckled. "Naw, Vicky, this is all baby fat."

Their laughter continued, filling the room with a sense of camaraderie that transcended the years they had spent apart.

As the laughter subsided, Vicky took a step back and gestured towards the man who had accompanied them. "Johnnie, this is Pastor Chad," she introduced. "Pastor Chad, this is John and Suzzette's son."

Pastor Chad, a calm and compassionate presence, extended his hand towards Johnnie. "It's a pleasure to meet you, Johnnie," he said.

Johnnie shook the pastor's hand, feeling a sense of comfort in the gentle grip. "Likewise," he replied, his eyes filled with gratitude.

With introductions made and greetings exchanged, they settled into the room, ready to catch up and share their stories. Little did they know that this reunion would set in motion a journey of faith, healing, and rediscovery that would change their lives forever.

Pastor Chad's words hung in the air like a soothing melody. "It's a pleasure to meet you," he said to Johnnie with a warm smile.

Johnnie, reciprocated the sentiment. "The same here," he replied, his voice filled with genuine appreciation.

Their eyes shifted toward the figure in the bed, Johnnie, whose face bore the marks of recent struggle. Suzzette, his mother, approached the bedside with a tender smile, her hand reaching out to rub his hair and plant a loving kiss on his forehead.

Pastor Chad, sensing the gravity of the situation, proposed, "Would you all like to say a prayer?"

A unanimous "yes" resonated through the room, and they gathered around the bed, joining hands. Pastor Chad took the lead.

"Lord," he began, his voice calm and reassuring, "your Word speaks promises of healing and restoration, and I thank you for the miracles you still perform today. Today I claim those promises over John. We believe in the healing power of faith and prayer, and we ask you to begin your mighty work in the life of John. Please reach down and surround him with supernatural peace and strength, and give Suzzette the faith to believe that all things are possible for those who believe. Protect John from Satan's lies and discouragement, and let his miraculous healing begin. In Jesus' name, Amen."

Suzzette, her eyes glistening with tears, whispered her gratitude, "Thank you so much, Pastor Chad."

The pastor smiled warmly. "You're welcome anytime, Suzzette."

Suzzette nodded, her heart uplifted by the collective faith in the room.

However, their peaceful moment was disrupted when police officers entered the hospital room. Suzzette's face contorted in confusion and concern. "What's going on?" she asked.

Officer Kirk, cleared his throat and spoke, "Evidence has come back that John's Blue 2010 Chevy pickup truck was involved in the hit-and-run accident that killed Stephenson's family dog, Scooby. We have captured video footage from a street camera showing his blue pickup truck speeding up the road, veering over the curb, and hitting Scooby. He never stopped."

Suzzette's eyes widened in disbelief. She spoke with a hint of anger, "So you're telling me that you're just going to barge in here and accuse my husband without any evidence?"

Tensions rose in the room as the accusations hung in the air, casting a shadow over the fragile hope that had just been kindled through prayer.

Officer Peterson met Suzzette's questioning gaze with a composed demeanor. "We do have evidence, Mrs. Steinburg," he explained evenly.

Suzzette, her voice trembling with a mixture of anger and fear, implored, "So can you please explain to me why my husband is being arrested? Whatever happened to having a little decency, for heaven's sake? My husband is lying here in a coma."

Officer Kirk spoke with a hint of sympathy in his tone, "We're not arresting anyone today, Mrs. Steinburg. We're going to give him time to recover, so we can see what happened the day Scooby was hit."

Suzzette, still bewildered, pressed for answers, "No one has still explained the reason why my husband is being accused."

Officer Peterson leaned forward slightly, his expression earnest as he clarified, "Mrs. Steinburg, if you hit a dog and stop, we'd go out and make a record of it. There's generally no arrest. But, if you hit a dog and you don't stop, that's where the issue arises. You have to stop and call the police. The big issue is the failure to stop to render aid. Mr. Steinburg did not stop."

Suzzette absorbed this information, her anger gradually giving way to a mix of concern and understanding. Officer Kirk continued, "In general, if you stop and make a reasonable effort to help the animal, the legal responsibility for the accident will not fall on you, but on the owner for allowing the dog to run loose."

Officer Peterson, sensing the emotional toll this revelation had taken on Suzzette and the fragile state of her family, offered a sincere apology. "We're very sorry for what happened to Mr. Steinburg, and we hope that he gets better."

With that, the Officers made their exit, leaving Suzzette and her family to grapple with the newfound knowledge of the incident involving Johnnie's truck. Their minds raced with questions, and an air of uncertainty settled over the hospital room.

CHAPTER TWENTY

A Web of Unfolding Events

Meanwhile, in Emily's house, the news played in the background, capturing Emily's mother's attention. Little did she know that the unfolding events would soon intersect with her own life, setting in motion a series of events that would test the bonds of faith, forgiveness, and redemption.

The NEWS REPORTER's voice filled the room, reporting on the hit-and-run accident involving a family's beloved dog, Scooby. Emily's mother couldn't help but turn up the volume as she listened to the details.

"The person responsible for the hit-and-run accident that killed a family's dog named Scooby," the reporter began, "his name is John Steinburg. He is the Senior Advisor for Mayor Cox. He is in critical condition following a severe car accident caused by driving under the influence of alcohol. Doctors have administered an induced coma due to the brain swelling. Police believe that alcohol may have played a huge factor in the death of Scooby. Alcohol was found in the truck when paramedics arrived on the scene."

With a heavy heart, Emily's mother switched off the television just as Emily returned home from school.

"Hi, honey, how was your day?" her mother asked as Emily hung up her backpack.

Emily let out a weary sigh. "It was a very long day, but it was okay. I can't wait until the weekend. Cassey's spending the weekend over. Her mother finally said yes."

Her mother mused, "I wonder what made her finally say yes."

But Emily's thoughts were elsewhere. "Mom, is Mrs. Steinburg's husband okay? All day during school, everyone has been talking about what happened to him. That he had a bad car accident and that he's in a coma. They even said he was the one who hit Scooby. Is that true?"

Emily's mother motioned for her to come closer. She took Emily's hand and explained, "Yes, honey, they believe he's the one responsible for Scooby's death. They traced back Mr. Steinburg's truck as the vehicle that killed Scooby. They are doing further investigations, okay? We don't just want to jump to any conclusions at this point until we get all the facts. Everyone is so ready to throw him under the bus, without giving him a chance."

Emily looked up at her mother with a determined expression. "Mom," she began, her voice filled with compassion and conviction, "I forgive Mr. Steinburg for killing Scooby. This is what God would want us to do. How can we listen to Pastor teach on forgiveness but not forgive? I don't want anyone throwing him under the bus. Scooby was my dog, and if I can forgive him, I know everyone else can. I want to go up to the hospital to see him."

Her mother regarded her daughter with a mixture of surprise and pride. "Emily, are you sure you want to do that?"

Emily nodded, her heart unwavering in its decision. "Yes, Mom. I want to show him that forgiveness is possible, even in the hardest of times."

Emily's determination shone brightly as she sat in the cozy living room of her home, engaging in a heartfelt conversation with her mother. The soft afternoon sunlight filtered through the curtains, casting a warm and comforting glow over their conversation. Emily's unwavering resolve was evident in her words.

"Mom, I'm sure. I want everyone to come up to the hospital with me and pray with Mr.

Steinburg. I want everyone to stop being mad at each other and forgive one another," Emily declared with conviction. Her young heart was burdened by the divisions she witnessed both at school and in their community, stemming from differences in political beliefs.

Emily's mother nodded, fully understanding her daughter's earnest plea.

"You are so absolutely right, honey. What do you need me to do to help? I've heard that some members of the community are still not speaking to each other."

Emily's eyes sparkled with hope as she voiced her ambitious plan.

"I want to go to the news and ask if everyone can come together again. I'm asking that the people of the Community of Hawthorne forgive one another. And just maybe, seeing them start to forgive one another will spread all across the world. But it has to start somewhere, and why not here?"

Her mother pondered her daughter's words before gently questioning her intentions.

"Honey, what are you expecting to get from all of this?" Emily gazed out the window, her thoughts reaching beyond their home.

"I'm expecting Scooby's death to not be in vain," Emily replied with unwavering determination. "I'm expecting something positive to come out of his death. Even if it has to start right here and spread like wildfire all across the world, the message that forgiveness is not just needed, it's necessary."

Her mother, moved by Emily's passion, came up behind her, wrapping her arm around her daughter's shoulders and planting a loving kiss on the top of her head.

"I'll call Pastor Chad so he can reach out to the community. I will also contact the news today. They've been trying to interview us for the longest time. We can have the news come to the hospital."

Emily's gratitude shone in her smile as she replied, "Thanks, Mom."

Her mother responded with a loving smile of her own, proud of her daughter's unwavering belief in the power of forgiveness and unity.

CHAPTER TWENTY ONE

A Message of Forgiveness and Unity

In the quiet hospital room, the noise from outside grew louder and more pronounced. Suzzette, curiosity piqued, moved toward the window, her gaze fixed on the commotion beyond.

"What's all the racket going on out there?" Suzzette wondered aloud.

The scene outside painted a vivid picture. A news truck stood parked, its satellite dish towering into the sky. A reporter, identified as Christa Main from Channel 10 News, was positioned in front of the hospital, ready to broadcast. The community had gathered, forming a circle, their clasped hands creating a powerful symbol of unity and hope.

Emily's parents and Pastor Chad stood nearby, offering their unwavering support. Inside their homes, people watched the news on their televisions, while others listened intently on their cell phones, the story reaching far and wide.

Christa Main's voice filled the room, drawing everyone's attention as she commenced her report. The focus of her story was the hit-and-run accident that had taken Scooby's life and put Mr. Steinburg in a coma. Alcohol was suspected to have played a significant role in the tragic event, a fact that had gripped the entire community.

Suzzette, on the other hand, had turned on the television to Channel 10 News, joining countless others in witnessing the unfolding events. Emily, surrounded by loved ones, clutched a card and teddy bear intended for Mr. Steinburg, ready to share her heart.

As Emily began to speak, she expressed her profound gratitude to the news team and her family for their support during these challenging times. Her words carried an air of forgiveness and a plea for unity. Emily believed that forgiveness was a crucial step towards healing, as she shared her perspective on the importance of this act in the eyes of God.

Suzzette couldn't hold back her tears as she listened to Emily's heartfelt message, her own emotions echoing the sentiment of the crowd gathered outside.

Christa Main, the news reporter, was visibly moved by Emily's words, her eyes glistening with tears. She embraced Emily, a symbol of their shared humanity and hope.

With the reporter's gentle encouragement, Emily's parents, Mr. and Mrs. Stephenson, stepped forward to convey their decision not to press charges against Mr. Steinburg. They entrusted the situation to a higher power, placing their faith in a greater plan.

As Suzzette wept, her son Johnnie offered his comfort through a warm embrace, acknowledging the significance of this moment.

The scene transitioned to the community, who arrived in a procession of cars at the hospital, ready to stand in solidarity with Emily and the Steinburg family. Emily, accompanied by Pastor Chad, her parents, Cassey, and others, walked into the room where Mrs. Steinburg awaited them.

"Hello, Mrs. Steinburg," Emily greeted, and the two women embraced, their shared pain and hope forging an unbreakable connection. The hospital room was filled with a sense of hope and unity as a group of people gathered around, their eyes focused on a small table beside a patient's bed. Emily, a young girl with a heart full of forgiveness, broke the silence.

"Thank you for allowing us to come and pray for Mr. Steinburg," she expressed with gratitude.

Suzzette, a gracious host in this difficult situation, replied with warmth, "It's a pleasure."

With a gentle concern, Emily asked, "Is it okay to take this over to him?" Suzzette glanced at the card and teddy bear on the table and back at Emily with a reassuring smile.

"That's a silly question, sure," she replied, eliciting laughter from the gathering.

Emily moved gracefully to the bedside of Mr. John Steinburg, the man who had unwittingly become a focal point of forgiveness and healing. She carefully placed the card and teddy bear on the table next to him before standing by his side.

"Hi, Mr. Steinburg," Emily began. "This is Emily. I brought you a teddy bear and a card. I hope you like it. I don't know if you can hear me or not. But I wanted to tell you that I forgive you for hitting Scooby. And I also want you to know that something amazing has come out of this tragedy, whether we believe it or not. You have so many people who care about you and are all surrounding your bedside, believing in God to heal you."

A glimmer of movement in John Steinburg's eyes caught Emily's attention. She turned her gaze towards the window, where she saw a heartwarming sight. People from all walks of life had gathered outside, holding hands, and offering prayers.

"Come look, guys, this is absolutely amazing!" Emily exclaimed, her voice filled with awe.

Everyone present in the room joined her by the window, witnessing the profound display of unity and compassion outside. Emily's mother wrapped her arms around her daughter as they stood there, sharing the moment.

Pastor Chad, a pillar of strength in their community, couldn't help but marvel at the scene. "Look at God! Well, let's gather together and pray."

The group of friends and family members encircled John Steinburg's bedside, forming a circle of faith and hope. Pastor Chad turned to Emily with a smile.

"Emily, do you want to lead the prayer?"

Emily's face lit up with excitement as she nodded, eager to convey her heartfelt prayer to the heavens.

"Thank you, Father, for your gift of forgiveness," Emily began, her voice filled with sincerity. "Your only Son loved us enough to come to earth and experience the worst pain imaginable so we could be forgiven".

Your mercy flows to us in spite of our faults and failures. Your Word says to 'clothe yourselves with love, which binds us all together in perfect harmony' (Col. 3:14). Help us demonstrate unconditional love today, even to those who may have hurt us. I pray that you heal Mr. Steinburg, Almighty Lord."

As Emily continued to pray, her words resonated with a sense of unity and healing. She reached out to the Divine, asking for restoration and recovery, not only for John Steinburg but for their entire community.

"Cover Mr. Steinburg with your sovereign hand," Emily implored, "bring restoration and healing to his body. I also ask that you bring healing, forgiveness, and restoration to our communities, families, nations, and all across the world, in Jesus' Name. Amen!"

In unison, everyone present in that hospital room, standing around John Steinburg's bed, echoed a heartfelt "Amen." It was a moment of profound togetherness, faith, and the beginning of a journey towards forgiveness and healing that would extend far beyond the walls of that room.

CHAPTER TWENTY TWO

A Time for Healing and Forgiveness

As time passed, the hospital became a place of hope and healing for John Steinburg. John was on the road to recovery, with Emily visiting him regularly. The small gestures of kindness, prayer, and forgiveness had a profound impact on his healing journey.

One sunny day, Johnnie, his son, made his way to the hospital room. John Steinburg was sitting by the window, reading his Bible, his reading glasses perched on his nose.

"Come in," John called out as Johnnie knocked on the door.

Johnnie entered, concerned but relieved to see his father in better spirits. He walked over to the bedside and asked, "Hi Dad, how are you feeling?"

"I'm feeling great," John replied, bookmarking his Bible. "I was reading Hosea 6:1. It says, 'Come, let us return to the LORD. He has torn us to pieces but he will heal us; he has injured us but he will bind up our wounds.'"

Johnnie reflected on the scripture and shared his thoughts. "Wow, God has His arms open for us to return to Him. If you really look at our own lives, we've been broken in so many ways by God just so that He can bring us to that place where we need Him to put us back together again and heal us. I think that is so amazing."

John nodded in agreement. "Yes, son, God is so amazing like that."

After a moment of quiet contemplation, John continued, "Johnnie, I'm so sorry for how I treated you and your mother. I only wanted the best for both of you, but I had an alcoholic problem. I allowed what my father did to my mother to affect my life with my family, and I shouldn't have allowed that."

Johnnie comforted his father, saying, "You shouldn't have to blame yourself. It's not your fault that Grandpa treated you and Grandmom the way that he did."

"I know," John acknowledged, "I just want our relationship to get better. I love your mother so much, and I love you."

"I love you too, Dad," Johnnie reassured him. "God has forgiven you, who am I not to forgive you? I forgive you, Dad. I thank God for you, Dad! You are the best Dad in the whole wide world."

John and Johnnie shared a heartfelt moment of forgiveness and reconciliation, their laughter filling the room.

Three Weeks Later

Outside Emily's front porch, a surprise awaited her. A puppy, adorned with a bow, had been delivered. Emily's mother answered the door, discovering the unexpected gift. Excitement radiated from Emily as she rushed downstairs to see.

"Who's at the door?" she inquired with curiosity.

"It's more like 'what' is at the door," her mother replied with a smile, undoing the bow.

"Who is it from?" Emily's anticipation grew.

"Your guess is as good as mine," her mother remarked as she uncovered the adorable puppy inside the box.

"Wow! A puppy!" Emily exclaimed, her excitement evident. She picked up the puppy, gently rubbing its soft fur.

As her mother opened a note that had accompanied the puppy, Emily continued to interact with her new furry friend.

"Dear Emily," her mother read aloud, "you have forgiven me, and I want to thank you. But I haven't asked you to forgive me for bringing so much hurt to your family. I hope that this gift shows you a token of how much I appreciate you. I really hope you like the puppy. From Mr. and Mrs. Steinburg."

"I love the gift! Thank you, Mr. and Mrs. Steinburg," Emily exclaimed, her heart warmed by this gesture of reconciliation.

Three Weeks Later

The passage of time brought about significant changes for everyone involved. Mr. Steinburg, now in a wheelchair, Johnnie, and Emily attended a church service together. The once-divided community now gathered as one, singing, clapping, and praising God.

Emily sat beside Mr. Steinburg, their smiles reflecting the newfound harmony and forgiveness that had transformed their lives. They shared a silent moment, appreciating the bond that had formed through trials and healing.

The church service continued, with the entire congregation rejoicing in the power of forgiveness, unity, and faith, a testament to the profound change that had taken root in the hearts of all those who had come together in the face of adversity.